How to Preach with an Interpreter

How to Preach with an Interpreter

A Crash Course

Dennis E. Bills

RESOURCE *Publications* • Eugene, Oregon

HOW TO PREACH WITH AN INTERPRETER
A Crash Course

Resource Publications
An Imprint of Wipf and Stock Publishers
199 W. 8th Ave., Suite 3
Eugene, OR 97401

www.wipfandstock.com

ISBN 13: 978-1-60899-363-5

Manufactured in the U.S.A.

To my wife Kathi

Contents

Acknowledgements

FOR MENTORING ME DURING graduate school and influencing this small book, I would like to express my sincere gratitude to Dr. Christian Wei, founder and president of Chinese for Christ International, to Dr. Mark Lehman, gifted missionary and founder of Beachhead to a Billion, and to Mr. Gary Balius, a frequent and single-minded short-term missionary to China. For her help in the editing of the manuscript, I am grateful to Mrs. Lara Rodkey, a friend and literature instructor in Huntington, West Virginia.

Introduction

IMAGINE YOURSELF STANDING BEFORE a group of people in a foreign land. You do not know their language, and they do not know yours. Thankfully, a national who more or less knows both languages stands at your side. You share the podium space, centered at the pulpit, shoulder to shoulder. After you say a few words, the interpreter translates, imitating your tone, pace, and gestures. The two of you take turns doing this for the next forty-five minutes. If this sounds easy, you should know that preaching with an interpreter can be more difficult than most first-timers anticipate. If this sounds difficult, intimidating, or distracting, you should know that it does not have to be if you and the interpreter are properly prepared.

This crash course is intended for missionaries, interpreters, evangelists, traveling pastors, stateside ministers to internationals, and anyone else who wants to preach but does not know the language. You might be a missionary in language school, a pastor traveling overseas, or a short-termer on a summer mission trip. In any case, an interpreter will help you communicate as soon as your feet hit foreign soil.

Obviously, a successful cross-cultural ministry requires good communication. Romans 10:14 reminds us that none will hear the Gospel message if no one communicates it. The Scriptures also teach that if this communication is unclear, the entire preaching experience is wasted for both the preacher and the hearer:

> Even in the case of lifeless things that make sounds, such as the flute or harp, how will anyone know what tune is being played unless there is a distinction in the notes? Again, if the trumpet does not sound a clear call, who will get ready for

> battle? So it is with you. Unless you speak intelligible words with your tongue, how will anyone know what you are saying? You will just be speaking into the air. Undoubtedly there are all sorts of languages in the world, yet none of them is without meaning. If then I do not grasp the meaning of what someone is saying, I am a foreigner to the speaker, and he is a foreigner to me (1 Corinthians 14:7-11).

Although this passage deals with the use of language gifts in worship, the overarching principle also applies to today's cross-cultural preacher—clear communication is essential. This is why missionaries seek to learn the language in which they minister and why many use an interpreter until they do.

In order to help you communicate effectively, this crash course explains everything you should know to succeed. As difficult as your job may be, the intimidating and unnatural job of interpreting can be even more complex. Therefore, the course goes into great detail concerning the role of the interpreter. With this information, you can sympathize with the process, help out if problems arise, or perhaps even teach the skill "from scratch" if necessary. The course also surveys common problems that preachers and interpreters encounter and suggests simple, easy-to-apply solutions. Finally, it details a variety of interpreted ministries and some methods to get the best results.

I have based this course upon observations of and participation in hundreds of interpreted sermons over the course of several years. I believe I have seen the major mistakes that preachers and interpreters can make (I made most of them myself!), and I have tried to address these as comprehensively as possible. As far as I know, nothing else like this is in print—which is, of course, why I wrote it and why I hope it will aid your ministry.

1

The Role of the Preacher

THE PREACHER'S CHIEF CONCERNS when using an interpreter ought to be 1) communicating with the interpreter, 2) maintaining a clear flow of thought, and 3) keeping the audience's attention. The ease or difficulty of these will depend on the skill of the interpreter, but the preacher can do his part to make the interpreted experience as smooth as possible.

COMMUNICATE WITH THE INTERPRETER

When preaching with an interpreter, realize that you are communicating with the interpreter as well as the audience. This communication should take place before, during, and after the sermon.

Before the Sermon

Before the sermon, the preacher should allow sufficient time for the interpreter to review the text and outline of the message. If possible, he should contact the interpreter to schedule a time when both can preview the content of the sermon together. Unless the interpreter is extremely skilled, he should not enter the pulpit without some idea of what the preacher will be talking about. The amount of time necessary for this will depend upon both the preacher's and the interpreter's ability and experience.

If neither has time to meet, perhaps the preacher could provide an outline of the sermon in advance. I say "outline" because, in my experience, interpreters who prepare with manuscripts are sometimes tempted to over-familiarize themselves with the material, in some cases to the point of memorization. Interpreters who over-prepare or memorize portions of the sermon may be thrown for a loop when you inevitably go off-script. Since preachers rarely speak from rote memory, the interpreter should be prepared to speak extemporaneously as well. Outlines provide the idea and direction of the sermon without giving the exact wording. If an outline is impractical, at least provide the text of the sermon so that the interpreter can look it up beforehand.

Additional help may be necessary if the sermon is technically or logically rigorous. Sometimes theological words are so technically precise that the interpreter needs to look them up. It might be helpful to anticipate and list complex theological terms and concepts so that the interpreter won't be caught off guard in the pulpit.

During the Sermon

Communication *during* the sermon is necessary when the interpreter has not understood what the preacher has said. The preacher should discern when the interpreter is struggling and should learn to repeat or rephrase sentences without being asked. Listen carefully for silence, stuttering, or requests for repetition from your interpreter. If you preach with an interpreter often, this will happen from time to time. When the interpreter is obviously struggling, avoid looking at or drawing attention to him. If he asks you to repeat yourself, do not turn to him and explain "in private." Rather, repeat or restate the sentence for all to hear, perhaps using different or simpler word choices. If, after a second try, the interpreter still does not understand the statement, try to minimize the awkwardness of the situation by simply moving on to the next thought.

For less formal occasions like Bible studies or Sunday school lessons, the dignity of moment may be less crucial. In these circumstances, you might feel freer to explain things directly to the interpreter so that he can in turn explain to the audience. Whatever the circumstances, you should both work hard to keep the interpreting process from being tedious and distracting.

Experienced interpreters can often handle such awkward situations without all these "rules." They can be smooth, entertaining, and calming. However, do not be surprised when even experienced interpreters misunderstand the preacher. I worked with one excellent translator who never "missed a beat" when a preacher said something he did not understand. Instead, he creatively translated what he thought the preacher might have said. Over the course of the next few sentences, he filled in any gaps. Rarely did he ever stop to have the preacher repeat himself. Most of the time, no one really noticed that he was covering for his lack of understanding. Most interpreters do not start with this level of ability but can get better with time and experience.

After the Sermon

Communication *after* the sermon is also important, especially for novice interpreters. You can discuss mistakes and theological issues to produce better mutual understanding, encourage each other, and simply work towards knowing each other better. Often, the better you know each other, the smoother and more profitable your ministry will be.

MAINTAIN A CLEAR FLOW OF THOUGHT

Do not underestimate the importance of maintaining a clear flow of thought throughout the sermon. A disorganized or poorly prepared sermon can be a nightmare for you, the interpreter, and the audience. Start with a clear proposition and make certain your primary points support it. Throw your neatly alliterated sermons out the window, because niftiness is entirely irrelevant when translated into another language. Do not play any tricks with language or try to impress. Stick with a clear, simple, well-ordered outline.

Remember that long and complex statements can jam the works. This is especially true when a preacher lists several items in a row, produces compound sentences, or does not pause between sentences. Statements can sometimes be so long or complex that the interpreter may forget the beginning by the time the end comes around. When this happens, the interpreter may ask the preacher to repeat himself, or he may translate the sentence in a way that loses important details.

To avoid this, capture the flow of your thoughts into concise, pregnant sentences. Each should be grammatically and conceptually simple and complete. A *grammatically* simple sentence consists of a subject-verb-object construction. Instead of using a compound sentence (two independent clauses, each containing a subject-verb-object construction, joined together by a conjunction), use two separate sentences, allowing time between each for interpretation. Similarly, a *conceptually* simple sentence contains a single idea. It is very tempting to pack as much meat into a sentence as possible, but that may be to the detriment of the interpreting process.

On the other hand, some preachers simplify too much by breaking sentences down into incomplete phrases or fragments. For example, suppose a preacher says the phrase, "Christians must remember that there are three ways, . . ." and then stops for the interpretation. The interpreter does his best with that half. In the next turn, the preacher finishes the sentence with "to devote themselves to prayer." Because the interpreter has been given two conceptual fragments, he may not be able to interpret sensibly in his turn. Sometimes the structure of languages is so different that it is difficult to compose sentences in the receptor language without having the complete thought all at once. Again, the grammar of the language may require a complete thought in order to construct a proper sentence. When an interpreter faces such a sentence (and it *will* happen), he will usually try to frame a sensible fragment with just the information that he has been given. When he hears the rest, he will probably repeat the first part in order to give the thought continuity. As one can imagine, this is inefficient and frustrating for both the listener and the interpreter.

The temptation for the preacher to break up sentences is usually strongest with "if . . . then" or "because this, this is true" statements. For instance, the following sentence can be broken into two different clauses at the slash: "Since the Bible was written by more than 40 different authors over a period of more than 1500 years with amazing continuity / we can trust that it is a divine book." An interpreter might, for instance, translate the first clause well but *forget* the causal relationship by the time the second clause comes around. The result is that the interpreter may struggle to translate the second clause. For the inexperienced interpreter's sake, the preacher should avoid using compound sentences whenever possible. The best way to accomplish this is to use simple and complete subject-verb-object constructions.

A Word about Scripture Reading

The problems I have just described make this a good place to discuss reading Scripture passages publically. The preacher will have two occasions to read Scripture during a sermon. The first is the initial reading of the text when introducing a sermon. As a rule of thumb, the interpreted preacher should read the entire passage in English from beginning to end without stopping for interpretation. Afterward, the interpreter should read the complete passage in his language. Reading, interpreting, and listening to long passages sentence by sentence or verse by verse can be excruciatingly tedious. Besides this, "stopping places" in one language are not always parallel to "stopping places" in another. Stopping and starting when reading Scripture can result in confusion and redundancy. You should allow the listener to hear the Word of God in his or her own language without distracting sentence, verse, or paragraph breaks.

The need to repeat a verse or phrase during the course of a sermon provides the second occasion for Scripture reading. Preachers do this when pulling points or sub-points from the text. Once again, the rule of thumb is to read complete verses, or at least sentences, whenever possible. Avoid stopping after reading only a portion of a sentence or verse. The nature of languages and their differing syntaxes may make it difficult for the interpreter to leave off and pick up exactly where you do. Instead, read whole sentences, verses, or paragraphs when possible. Anything less may create confusion for the audience and the interpreter.

KEEP THE AUDIENCE'S ATTENTION

Frankly, an interpreted sermon has the potential to be really, really boring. Don't underestimate how difficult it is to keep an audience's attention while preaching with an interpreter. Several "boredom factors" contribute to this phenomenon.

The first is the simple fact that interpreted sermons take longer to preach. The interpreter will usually need the same amount of time you did in order to interpret your words (and sometimes more). This means that the length of an interpreted sermon will at least be doubled. The obvious implication is that normal sermons need to be cut in half. If 30 minutes is allotted for the message, prepare 15 minutes of material. Even then, interpreted sermons will often go longer than planned. The need to repeat phrases, clarify statements, and explain concepts tends to draw out sermons.

Another boredom factor is the sermon's "pause-preach-pause-preach" rhythm. This rhythm naturally reduces the audience's ability to focus. God has designed the mind to follow a clear and straightforward flow of thought with relative ease. However, consistent interruptions by another language can lull the mind and cause attention to suffer. A "pause-preach" rhythm *in combination with* long sermons is deadly to all but the most respectful of audiences.

An additional "boredom" factor is the interpreter's language limitations. Even if the interpreter knows English well, he may not register the nuances of language that preachers use to capture attention. We spend years honing our ability to thrill the mind using language alone (so we tell ourselves). However, the preacher's descriptive illustrations and flowery, detailed language can be instantly lost on an interpreter. Suppose I use the phrase "flowery, descriptive, detailed language" in a sermon. My interpreter will likely struggle to voice three distinct, yet somewhat synonymous adjectives in the receptor language. Instead, he will probably reduce my adjectives down to basically equivalent words, such as "fancy language" or something similar. For this reason, let go of your attachment to big words and fancy expressions. You will not be able to count on your verbal abilities to keep your audience's attention.

Frequent illustrations may help greatly, but don't count on their *descriptive* nature to capture an international audience's attention. Instead, try to focus on the *action* of the illustration. If possible, avoid using abstract analogies—not because the audience is unintelligent (never presume this no matter how "third-world" your audience may be!), but simply because interpreted sermons can be tedious. Rather than "still" pictures, attempt to give your listeners an action to reproduce in their minds. Instead of snap-shots, give them video. Stories will usually alleviate boredom better than abstractions and complex metaphors.

The most effective anti-boredom technique is good teamwork. Teamwork takes practice and experience for both preachers and interpreters. Meanwhile, preachers can combat boredom factors by keeping points focused and to a minimum, speaking clearly and straightforwardly, and keeping the sermon as short as possible. Fifteen to twenty minutes of sermon content is a good goal for many situations. Obviously, if you are in one of those rare countries where people will sit for hours and peer through windows to hear preaching in packed houses, you should take as much time as you need. Don't kid yourself though—they are probably just being polite. It's a cultural thing.

2

The Role of the Interpreter

THE INTERPRETER HAS BEEN jokingly called "the interrupter." Pastors who have been invited to preach in another country will hopefully be provided an experienced and skilled "interrupter." However, visiting speakers do not always have that luxury. In order to do less "interrupting" and more powerful, effective interpreting, the interpreter should accurately communicate the speaker's meaning, naturally capture the preacher's delivery style, and practice, practice, practice. Preachers who understand this intimidating and difficult task can make the translator's job interesting and enjoyable.

COMMUNICATE THE PREACHER'S MEANING

When trying to communicate the speaker's meaning, nothing substitutes for a good knowledge of the language. Obviously, the interpreter should have some mastery of both the receptor language and the source language. Someone who is limited in English will have limited ability to interpret. I have at times preached in situations where interpreters were either not skilled in English or not skilled in the receptor language. Either way, the sermons turned into fatiguing events for everyone.

As the interpreter strives to accurately communicate the speaker's meaning, he must quickly perceive it and then convert it into the target language. The interpreter accomplishes this in two ways. First, he can translate *word for word* as grammar and vocabulary allow. This requires fast thinking and talking and is typically the ideal when possible.

The second way is to *paraphrase* the meaning of the speaker. When paraphrasing, the interpreter explains the preacher's sentences rather than translating them word for word. This is necessary when the speaker uses unusually long sentences or series of sentences (which, unfortunately for the interpreter, every speaker does occasionally). When the interpreter hears long sentences, he may comprehend their meaning but forget their exact wording. He will then explain in his own words the meaning that he has comprehended. Although this freestyle can take away from the unique delivery of the speaker, it is sometimes perfectly appropriate and often even necessary. I observed this in China when a house church was gathered together one evening to discuss a Bible lesson with me. As they asked questions, I gave some lengthy responses. One of the men then turned to the others and took a minute or two to explain. He did not try to interpret word for word, but first comprehended what I was saying and then put it all into his own words. This style of interpreting is best for informal occasions, such as Bible studies or discussion classes.

A balance between literal and free translation is best. An interpreter can err by being either too literal or too free. Novice interpreters will often have problems striking the balance. Those who attempt to translate very literally often experience frustration at not being able to communicate as quickly and fluently as they would like. They are stilted and halting because they are constantly trying to find the most equivalent words. On the other hand, those who are very free in their method of translation risk a lack of precision. They tend to generalize statements and minimize the personality and style of the preacher during the sermon. Vague terms and descriptions will often detract from the very exacting task of preaching the Word of God. The interpreter should seek balance through practice and experience.

Occasionally an interpreter may overstep his bounds by interjecting personal comments or explanations into the sermon. This is most likely to happen if you and the interpreter have worked together often, know each other well, and are comfortable with each other. Familiarity and ease may cause an interpreter to take liberties. Once when I was conducting a Bible study to about a dozen people, my interpreter paused in his translation to challenge my interpretation of a passage. Not only was it embarrassing, it was counterproductive to the purposes of the Bible study. Unless the format is an open discussion, it is generally better for the interpreter to wait until after the study to express personal opinions. If you are responsible for training the interpreter, encourage him to save any commentary for open discussions.

CAPTURE THE PREACHER'S DELIVERY STYLE

In addition to accurately communicating the meaning of the speaker, the interpreter should also capture the preacher's delivery style. When the speaker gestures specifically, so should the interpreter. When the speaker raises or lowers his voice for emphasis, the interpreter should follow suit. For the few minutes that the speaker and interpreter are in front of the audience, the interpreter should consider himself an extension of the speaker—the interpreter is the speaker in a different language. His job is to relay the words, gestures, and emphases of the one who is speaking.

I should warn that this may from time to time result in unexpected but usually harmless humor. When the interpreter begins imitating your every action, it can sometimes be funny. If this is not intentional, it can ruin a good point. Many times, I have observed a smirk in the audience as someone attempts to hold back a giggle during a serious part of the sermon. Sometimes, however, this humor can be good. For instance, a speaker might tell a humorous illustration in which he uses a gesture and jumps up and down vigorously. As the interpreter imitates the preacher's antics, it will no doubt cause a snicker or two. In these circumstances, the audience has just enjoyed seeing the speaker do something very funny and anticipates the interpreter's doing the same. It would probably be suitable to gratify them. Remember that interpreted sermons can be tedious, and humor can sometimes alleviate this. However, be careful that this does not get out of hand. The interpreter should not consciously produce humor if it is not intended by the speaker or suitable for the circumstances. As the interpreter seeks to reflect the delivery style of the preacher, he does not need to do so at the cost of his or the occasion's dignity. Through it all, both preacher and interpreter should attempt to remain natural and dignified.

PRACTICE! PRACTICE! PRACTICE!

Very few novices can convert English into another language without struggling. Just like the preacher, the interpreter's job is aided by training that ideally begins before he ever stands in front of an audience. Hopefully, he has had the opportunity to observe good interpreting. Perhaps he has been able to practice in his mind, checking his translation against that given by the interpreter. Even this, however, will not give the trainee the skill he needs to stand in the pulpit. Several potential interpreters have told me, "While I was in my seat listening to the sermon, I interpreted everything perfectly in my head. But when I stood up in front of people, for some reason, I could not do it smoothly." Something about being in front of an audience unsettles the minds of novices and flusters them into stumbling and apprehension. Fortunately, improvement comes with time and practice.

In Bible colleges, seminaries, and graduate schools across the country, students spend hours every semester learning how to preach. Their homiletics courses can go so far as to teach them how to move their hands, vary their pace, and raise and lower their voices at appropriate moments. Interpreters can benefit from similar training and practice. In my own ministry, I occasionally taught the skill of interpreting by offering short seminars on the subject. Using an experienced interpreter, I gave a brief sample of what a good interpreted sermon should sound like before allowing a daring soul to give it a try. After five minute training sessions, class members helped analyze what aspects of his interpreting needed improvement. Some readers may remember similar peer criticism in their own homiletics classes.

Formal classes with an experienced interpreter are probably not practical for most people, but a potential interpreter can still benefit from informal practice. Try spending some time together practicing one-on-one. Even without someone to correct him, the simple experience of interpreting can go a long way toward smoothing out the process. The novice will probably recognize many of his own mistakes and work to correct them.

To help potential interpreters develop skills and become more confident, start small by assigning them smaller roles in worship services like interpreting announcements, leading the singing, or doing Scripture readings. They can also interpret Bible studies, small Sunday school classes, or other less formal events. Regardless of the method of instruction, most students will find that simple practice makes a huge difference.

3

Problems in an Interpreted Ministry

I HAVE ALREADY DESCRIBED many problems that interpreted ministries often face. Here, though, is a more detailed list of problems, along with some suggested solutions. All my suggestions originate in mistakes that I have either observed or personally made.

MISCOMMUNICATION

The most obvious difficulty that an interpreted ministry faces is the possibility of miscommunication. The preacher is very dependent upon an interpreter's ability to understand English. If the interpreter does not grasp your meaning, he will have a very difficult time relaying it to the audience. Even if he knows English well, the risk of miscommunication still increases when speaking through an interpreter. The fact is that your presentation is "once-removed" from the source, and like a copy of a copy, it is possibly less clear than you intend it to be.

Since translation filters a preacher's communication abilities, you should humbly remember that the content of a sermon is more important than the way it is delivered. After spending years honing presentation skills to the supposed "oooh-and-ahh" level, an interpreted ministry takes preachers back to square one. In the target language, you will probably never be able to communicate with the skill that you can in your first language. This forces simplicity and dependence upon the Holy Spirit. No more ostentatious or stylistically impressive sermons. The content of the sermon is supremely important. The style and artistry of the sermon is not.

Many times I have had people come to me after a sermon to question me about something that was not communicated clearly. On one occasion, I told an illustration that was apparently misunderstood by my interpreter. I was explaining God's burden for the various people-groups of the world. To illustrate, I mentioned that I sat in my living room one night with all the lights off, except for the light inside a world globe on the mantle. As I turned my head to look out the living room window into the dark of the night, I saw the globe reflecting in the windowpane. From my position on the couch, it looked as though the earth was floating in the darkness of space. For a brief moment, I imagined that I saw the earth as God might see it. Sorrow filled my heart as I beheld an entire world that needed Christ. I thought it was a touching illustration. Unfortunately, my interpreter simply said that I saw the earth floating in the sky while I was looking out my window one day. The confused congregation ended up thinking I was a little strange.

This was only a minor problem. If the interpreter does not have a good grasp of theological words in both languages, the risk of miscommunication greatly increases. Without proper theological terminology on hand, the sermon loses accuracy and conciseness. Many times I have had to answer questions after the sermon because of such imprecision. To prevent this, either avoid using a novice interpreter for complex subjects or radically simplify the presentation. Such miscommunication is not always the interpreter's fault. The preacher ought to work very hard to make certain he is understandable. Preach as simply as is necessary to guarantee that the interpreter can translate accurately.

SERMON LENGTH AND PREPARATION TIME

The extended length of interpreted sermons will sometimes be a problem. All of us have heard stories of Gospel-starved countries where people are willing to sit for hours to listen to guest preachers. Some of us may have even experienced this. However, most of us should not presume that our listeners are so gracious. Since sermons will be twice as long, the material brought to the pulpit should be half as long. What is only a 30 minute sermon in English—fairly short by most standards—will become a 60 minute sermon when translated. Earlier I made the point that interpreted sermons are already difficult to listen to, and that when they are longer than normal, they will be more likely to bore listeners. Most preachers recognize that audiences can appreciate up to forty or forty-five minutes of sermon time. In keeping with this standard, consider preparing approximately twenty minutes of material for a total of forty to forty-five minutes of presentation time.

Short sermons can create another problem for the preacher. Well-developed and simply-stated material can require significant preparation time. A prominent preacher of considerable exegetical ability once told me that he spends more time preparing for a twenty-five minute chapel message than for a one hour, Sunday evening sermon. He realized that when he had less time, quality was more important than quantity. It is hard work for long-winded preachers to limit sermon time. Even after preparing adequately, you should still keep your eye on the clock and on the people. The audience's attention level can tell you if the sermon length is getting wearisome.

FEAR AND TIMIDITY

The mindset of inexperienced interpreters can be another problem. A fearful or bashful interpreter is a miserable interpreter. To overcome fear, the interpreter should prepare well, understand his indispensability, and be confident. All three of these are necessarily interrelated.

Preparation

Preparation goes a long way toward instilling confidence and bringing out natural abilities in the receptor language. The best way to prepare is to meet with the preacher beforehand, even if only for a moment. As I have already said, the preacher should allow sufficient time for the interpreter to review the text and outline of the message. If possible, he should contact the interpreter to schedule a time when both can preview the content of the sermon together. You might try providing the interpreter with an outline of the sermon well in advance of the occasion if opportunity permits. Regardless, it is not fair to send interpreters, especially inexperienced ones, into the pulpit without some idea of the sermon's content.

Once again, additional help may be necessary if the sermon will be technically or logically rigorous. Sometimes theological words used in messages are not a part of everyday communication. Do not assume that they are common knowledge. Words like *righteousness, justification*, *sanctification*, etc., are sometimes misunderstood in our own language. You can imagine how this possibility might increase in another. You may want to provide a list of any theological terms you know you will be emphasizing. The interpreter can then look up any unknown words in a dictionary and avoid being caught off guard or embarrassed in the pulpit.

Indispensability

In order to overcome fear, the interpreter should also understand that he is indispensable. The audience contains people who either do not understand English or who are limited in their understanding. What the interpreter says is not merely an afterthought to the preacher's words but is an important and essential part of the process. Without the interpreter, many or all would not understand the sermon. First Corinthians 14 gives validity to his ministry. Without him, preaching would be as a clanging cymbal or an imprecise trumpet call. It would be useless—mere sounds. Romans 10 reminds us that the lost cannot hear without a preacher.

I can recall one interpreter-in-training whose primary responsibility was to relay announcements to a mixed audience. Because many of the people in the audience understood English fairly well, he went into the pulpit believing that his interpretation was not really necessary. This influenced his attitude during the service and discouraged those of us who were in charge of the meeting (and his training). Sometimes he interpreted selectively and, every once in a while, not at all. This created confusion in the pulpit and in the pew. Aside from the fact that the experience would have been valuable for training's sake, several people in the audience were actually very limited in their knowledge of the English language. When an interpreter realizes his value in the communication process, his confidence in the pulpit naturally increases.

Boldness

Good preparation and an understanding of one's indispensability work together to give the interpreter the confidence necessary to perform the job with boldness. God has not given us a spirit of fear, but of power, love and a disciplined mind. Among other things, this adds up to boldness in the pulpit. The interpreter is a preacher just like the person for whom he is interpreting. He should stand in the pulpit, look at the congregation, and proclaim the Word of God with intensity and zeal. Many novices could do much to help their ministry by simply standing tall in the pulpit and speaking to the audience loudly and clearly. I can think of one young man who would sometimes hurry through his turn with an abbreviated translation. At the end of his sentences he would drop to such a low volume that I am sure no one else understood or even heard what he said. He lacked confidence and an understanding of just how essential his job was. If you have the opportunity to encourage timid interpreters, remind them of the value God places upon clear communication according to Romans 10 and 1 Corinthians 14. This reminder, combined with patience and practical experience, will build bolder interpreters.

Good preparation, a sense of indispensability, and confidence can only be developed with sufficient practice. Practice provides the experience necessary to help fearful and timid interpreters overcome the bashfulness of inexperience.

LOCATING INTERPRETERS

The last problem that I will mention is that skilled interpreters are hard to find. This is not because people are not capable of interpreting with practice, but because it is difficult to locate people with both the willingness and time to become effective. Almost anyone can turn to the person beside him or her and explain what the preacher just said, but it takes a person with the heart of a preacher to become an effective interpreter. The preacher should keep his eyes open for signs of giftedness in this area. It is possible for an interpreter to arise from among those who show potential for leadership in ministry. On the other hand, never underestimate what gifts and desires God may place in the hearts of the most unlikely people.

A good way to locate and train interpreters is through small group Bible study. Most church planters begin similarly. Over time, people are converted or begin attending regularly. Just as in a church plant, leaders eventually rise to the surface by God's providence. From these, interpreters may also arise. Be patient and pray for God to give you someone with a minister's heart.

4

Types of Interpreted Ministries

EVERY YEAR, THOUSANDS OF pastors and laymen take short-term mission trips to churches and communities in countries all over the world. These mission trips aim to accomplish a wide variety of ministries, many of which require interpreters. Interpreters are usually arranged in advance by missionaries on location. Often the missionaries themselves will interpret. Regardless of who does the job, the most effective interpreted ministries are those for which an interpreter is readily available. When activities are regularly scheduled or scheduled well in advance, an interpreter can more easily be arranged, which is why preaching is perhaps the most obvious interpreted ministry.

Teaching is very similar to preaching, except the audience is often smaller, more interactive, and the material covered is more academic by nature. Many stateside churches and seminaries sponsor classes in other countries in order to train nationals for ministry. These one or two week classes and seminars are often taught by visiting professors and preachers. This sort of work may require a teacher and interpreter to work together for long hours throughout the day. Leading small group Bible studies on regular occasions would also fit under this category. Both preaching and teaching are obviously similar in that they communicate to groups of people on regularly scheduled occasions. The regular nature of these activities makes an interpreter easier to schedule.

Organized evangelism is another activity that is sometimes regularly scheduled. After a sermon, for instance, the interpreter can be on hand to talk with those who may desire to hear more about the Gospel. If the ministry has regularly-scheduled visitation or community canvassing on certain nights of the week, then those involved can be paired with interpreters. Evangelism that occurs on the spur of the moment in the course of normal, daily activities is more difficult unless you know the language. This is more likely to be the domain of long-term missionaries who have settled into a community and already speak the language. Otherwise, you will find yourself witnessing mostly to people you encounter who also happen to speak your language.

Many mission trips are geared more toward community service than preaching and teaching. Churches send groups to other countries for one or two weeks to do activities like construction, painting, repairs, or sports camps. In these cases, someone is usually around who speaks the language and can interpret informally at the worksite. As long as the interpreter knows the languages, no special training or experience is necessary. On the other hand, medical missions may require a more skilled interpreter. Doctors, nurses, and laymen sometimes travel to help out in communities where illness is rampant and medical services are lacking. In those cases, it is crucial to have an interpreter who knows medical terms in both languages and can accurately describe symptoms and courses of treatment. Lives may depend upon having qualified interpreters. Regardless, all service-oriented mission teams often find themselves participating in "after hours" community evangelism and Bible studies. A broadly-skilled interpreter would be handy in those situations.

Many times an interpreted ministry is not practical, especially for the more irregular aspects of ministry such as emergencies, counseling, discipleship, and discipline. These are often scheduled at odd times and may come up in the spur of the moment. A minister cannot expect an interpreter to be available at all times of the day or night, and sometimes the sheer volume of these ministries make it impractical. Interpreters may be difficult to arrange, but perhaps you have access to an unusually committed helper who would be glad to be "on call."

Many who come for counseling have problems so private that an interpreter might be awkward. People who are struggling with sin seldom want others to know about it, so dealing with these on a one-on-one basis is obviously best. However, if English is limited, and no one else is available, then the session should be scheduled in advance so that a trusted interpreter can help with the counselee's permission. Such an occasion is no time for confusion. If the interpreter is mature enough and well-respected, you may want to consider allowing him or her to do the counseling.

Preachers will do well to teach people to minister for them in these more awkward circumstances. Remember that the best person to carry on a ministry will always be a trained national with whom people can identify. Consider the wisdom of teaching an interpreter to be a "first language" minister (one who speaks it as their primary language). A godly person, knowledgeable and full of integrity, can learn to minister on the preacher's behalf. You might even foresee that this person could someday replace you. You are, after all, attempting to work yourself out of a job. The time you spend with an interpreter preparing, preaching, and practicing can also serve as training for leadership. Many missionaries plan to hand their ministries over to nationals before going somewhere else to start from scratch. In the long run, a first language minister should be able to do a missionary's job better and with more extensive impact.

A NOTE FOR MISSIONARIES

Although this information was designed primarily for traveling pastors, short-termers, or those who minister to internationals within the United States, many who read this may be planning to be permanent missionaries on the foreign field. I hope this material is valuable for you in the early stages of your ministry. However, you should not allow yourself to get trapped by the supposed convenience of an interpreted ministry. An interpreted ministry will never substitute for the ability to speak the language yourself.

Some missionaries jump into busy ministry as soon as they get to the foreign field, keeping them from adequately learning the language. Tragically, some have been on the field for years and still cannot communicate well. Until a missionary has developed the ability to speak the local language, full-time ministry should probably be second priority. For most missionaries and missionary agencies, language school is the top priority. Many even go to language school in a location other than where they plan to minister in order to devote one hundred percent of their time to learning the language.

A NOTE FOR STATESIDE MINISTERS TO INTERNATIONALS

I have already hinted that an important part of ministry to internationals is a discipleship program. Even though an American minister can carry on a preaching and teaching ministry for years with an interpreter, he will never be as effective as a first language communicator. If you find this is the case in your ministry, you should pray for and seek out Christian leaders who can themselves become ministers in their own international communities. One of the first people to consider for this discipleship should probably be the interpreter. As I have already said, the time you spend with an interpreter preparing, preaching, and practicing can also serve as training for leadership. It is possible that your interpreter could develop into a very capable ministry aide or maybe even take over significant aspects of the ministry.

Ministries that rely entirely on interpreted preaching may eventually plateau or even stagnate. An elder from an international ministry once explained to me that his ministry had reached a point where it could no longer grow as a blended congregation. The tedium of interpreting had become a drawback. Once they put a first language minister into leadership and created two separate services, one in English and the other in the foreign language, the ministry again began to grow.

5

Overcoming Obstacles

WHETHER YOU ARE A short-term or long-term missionary, the fact that you are a foreigner and do not speak the language like the locals will always be an obstacle to successful ministry. This is true even if you become fluent in the target language, so it is even truer during the time that you minister using an interpreter. Even so, certain compensators can help an interpreted minister overcome these obstacles and increase the possibility of success. If a national minister is at the top of the ministerial ladder and an interpreted minister is at the bottom, the following compensators may help an interpreted minister climb the ladder a few rungs. They are common sense and should ring true for ministers in any culture.

The first compensator is required of all ministers in all cultures in order to be successful—*love*. According to I Corinthians 13, you can communicate in the target language, but if you do not have love, you are just making noises. Ministers who do not love their people are probably wasting everyone's time. Years ago, my seminary dean pounded this truism into his "preacher boys" again and again: "Some pastors may be awful preachers, disorganized, boring, or lacking social skills, but I have discovered this—if your people know you love them, they will overlook just about anything."

Years ago, a friend of mine gave nearly all his spare time to ministry among Chinese people here and abroad. He was nearly clueless as to how to relate to them, sometimes comically so. Once, when in China, some local Christians took us out to eat. Before the meal my friend told me confidently, "Just watch me and I will teach you their customs." After our waiter set out some shelled peanuts in a small dish, my friend immediately reached for them, grabbed a handful, and began popping them into his mouth. I watched our Chinese friends stare shocked and gape-jawed at this before one of them slowly picked up his chopsticks, pinched a single peanut, and slid it discretely into his mouth. I learned how to use chopsticks that day—I had to if I wanted a peanut. My friend was obviously not Chinese, though he tried his hardest to fit in. He could not speak the language, and he unwittingly transgressed more cultural customs than he ever knew. However, the people to whom he ministered knew that he loved them very much, and they listened to him and respected him for it.

A second set of compensators is *time and attention*. The more time and attention a minister gives to people, the more opportunities he has to convince them that what he has for them is real and valuable. Stopping to give someone extra attention, to look them in the eye (if it is culturally appropriate), to drop everything for the sake of a person's needs, to listen carefully, all work to overcome the problems inherent in an interpreted ministry.

A third set of compensators is *knowledge* and *experience*. Knowledge of the target culture proves that the minister is seeking to identify with people. A successful missionary friend once commented, "When the speaker cites an authority within the target culture (instead of Calvin or another Westerner) or expresses Christian doctrine in the framework of the target culture (instead of expressing Christianity in the format of a 'pioneer' spirit or from the perspective of an assumed Christian heritage), when the speaker exhibits a familiarity with target religions, or when the speaker demonstrates an accomplishment in some area of the target culture, people are more willing to listen." All this presupposes that the minister has knowledge of the culture to which he is ministering, and that he has cared enough to learn about life from their perspective. This may include simple things such as dress, stance, demeanor, and other customs and habits. Among the Chinese, for instance, double tap with the fingers on the table when someone pours tea to say "thank you"; pass items (including business cards) using both hands to show respect; dismiss compliments humbly; handle chopsticks respectfully; cover the mouth when using a toothpick, etc. Education in these sorts of cultural details will never end, but knowledge gained along the way will help the minister relate to and identify with people.

Knowledge of the language also goes a long way toward overcoming barriers. Obviously, a minister who knows the language does not need an interpreter, so once again we find a strong case for learning the language as soon as possible. However, those who are on whirlwind international preaching tours may find it very helpful at the least to learn some basic phrases in the target language. Learn to say "hello," "goodbye," "thank you," "you're welcome," and other common courtesies. Learn how to ask some basic questions, like "how much does this cost?" or "where can I find the bathroom?" When the opportunity arrives, show off a little. The way you say things will either make them laugh or impress them. Either way, they will appreciate the fact that you are trying to identify with them.

Experience produces respect in many cultures. Most cultures recognize the value of being an "elder." Unfortunately, the only thing that will give a younger minister more experience is, well, experience. In my younger years, my travels abroad helped me to overcome some of the disadvantages of youth. It was helpful to say, "Oh yes, I have been there," or "Is that where you're from? Isn't it such a beautiful city?!" Those to whom I ministered always smiled when I talked about having visited their own country or showed them pictures. Everyone's experience is different, but we each can eventually bring something to our ministries that can be of value when dealing with others.

Oddly enough, in some situations, the foreignness of *race* or *nationality* can be a compensator, particularly in countries where foreigners are rare. This appears counter-intuitive considering foreignness is what ministers are trying to overcome. An experienced missionary once explained, "In East Asia (and maybe elsewhere in the world), the fact that the speaker *is* white is a natural compensator. There is still some of the Great White Father image hanging over to a certain degree. Since Christianity is a 'Western' religion, it is reasonable to think that a Westerner would know more about it." Thus, being a foreigner can lend a natural authority in a culture that is curious to learn more about the West and its religion. In some cultures, it is easy for the strange, foreign preacher to gather a crowd.

Another compensator is *humor*. All cultures laugh, and not surprisingly, they often laugh at the same things that we do. While many jokes do not easily transfer into other languages, personal anecdotes, embarrassing experiences, and funny illustrations will cause people to smile the world over. Humor begets good will, and good will opens doors for ministry.

Of course, as our final and most essential compensator, we must acknowledge the *Holy Spirit*. God is very capable of overcoming all cultural disadvantages and incompatibilities. We know that the Holy Spirit integrally works in and through the words of preachers and in the hearts of recipients to bring about the salvation of people's souls. Without the Holy Spirit, any work would be in vain. We may plant, others may water, but God will give the increase.

Conclusion

Nearly any preacher can communicate by means of an interpreter. However, if you know ahead of time what you are getting into and have the time and opportunity to apply some of the suggestions found in this crash course, you can become a better, more effective communicator during your cross-cultural experience. Interpreting does not come naturally for most people and takes hard work on the part of both preachers and interpreters.

If and when you finally do get the opportunity to preach overseas, to take the Gospel to the regions beyond, to preach where no one else has preached, may God bless your endeavor for his sake. I hope you will preach the Word with power and excitement. And I hope that you will see fruit for your labors because of your willingness to preach to people using their own language.

> Undoubtedly there are all sorts of languages in the world, yet none of them is without meaning. If then I do not grasp the meaning of what someone is saying, I am a foreigner to the speaker, and he is a foreigner to me (1 Cor. 14:10–11).

Appendix

SECULAR APPLICATIONS: HOW TO SPEAK WITH AN INTERPRETER IN NON-RELIGIOUS CONTEXTS

EVERY DAY, COUNTLESS PEOPLE all over the world use interpreters in non-religious contexts. Businessmen and women gather around tables and negotiate contracts. They address stockholders and employees in business meetings and take potential clients out on the town. Educators participate in exchange programs with foreign universities, teaching classes and training, or being trained by other teachers. Charitable organizations send armies of altruistic men and women to other cultures to help them with medical needs, to construct buildings, or to teach English. Government diplomats meet to solve regional problems, to improve relations between countries and territories, and to negotiate agreements. As far as I know few if any resources exist to teach these people how to communicate using an interpreter. Thankfully, many organizations do have the resources to vet interpreters for experience and skill, making the secular speaker's job much easier. Not all speakers will be so lucky, and most would still benefit from a quick overview of the interpreted process.

In secular contexts, interpreting can be either formal or informal. Examples of informal interpreting might include social events, business meals, or entertainment. On any of these occasions, an interpreter might accompany you throughout the evening to help you communicate with those you meet. This requires little preparation on either part. However, if you get to know your interpreter, you will soon learn how complex your grammar and vocabulary should be. If your interpreter has a hard time conversing with you, this might be a clue that you are in for a difficult evening. However, if you can converse with ease and full, mutual understanding, you can probably relax and enjoy yourself.

Formal interpreting is quite different. You have probably observed one type, for example, in news reports of diplomatic speeches at the United Nations. The speaker is interpreted by a bank of translators broadcasting into earpieces. No one actually sees the interpreters since several may be translating from private booths at the same time. And since the speech is translated in "real-time," the speaker need not worry about being interrupted. These setups are rare and do not apply to most people.

More commonly, formal scenarios will resemble what this crash course has described. The presenter and interpreter stand before a group of people and take turns talking throughout the presentation. But even these circumstances can have a range of formality. For instance, some occasions might be less formal and more intimate and interactive, such as meetings in small classrooms, in homes, or at restaurants. Larger venues such as auditoriums or conference rooms will likely be more formal. The more formal the occasion, the more precise and technical the interpreter will attempt to be, using a sort of formal equivalence—word for word, gesture for gesture. On less formal, relaxed, and interactive occasions, the interpreter will probably translate using a more dynamic equivalence—explaining ideas and concepts in his or her own words with a view to ensuring that the audience is engaged and understanding.

The main body of this crash course contains suggestions for most occasions regardless of formality. Even though it was developed for religious purposes, a full reading of the material would benefit any interpreted speaker regardless of the situation. Much of it could be easily adapted for secular contexts with a few, quick, mental edits. Having said that, I will summarize some key points for quick-and-easy reference below. You will find more detailed explanations of each in the main body of the book.

QUICK-AND-EASY REFERENCE

- Before your presentation, supply the interpreter with an outline or script and review technical jargon.
- Be aware of the interpreter's performance during the presentation. If you perceive that he or she is struggling, slow down, construct simpler sentences, and explain difficult ideas. Speak to the audience and not to the interpreter.
- Debrief the interpreter following the presentation, especially if you will be working together again. Ask if he or she needs any further explanation or has any questions.
- Organize your presentation with a clear proposition or thesis statement and support it with points that are clearly related. Transition obviously from point to point using words like first…, second…, etc.
- Do not play language tricks (such as alliteration or puns) or try to impress anyone with your vocabulary or public speaking skills.
- Avoid long, complex statements and capture your flow of thought in concise, straightforward sentences. Avoid using compound sentences or throwing too many ideas into one sentence. Express whole sentences one at a time, avoiding sentence fragments.
- Be aware of time limits and plan accordingly. Since interpreted presentations are effectively doubled in length, prepare half as much material as the time allotted to you.
- Keep the interpreter's language limitations in mind. Interpreters might not comprehend the nuances of flowery, descriptive language, so use simple, straightforward words.
- Use interesting illustrations to prevent the boredom that frequently accompanies interpreted presentations. Stories usually alleviate boredom better than abstractions and complex analogies.

About the Author

Dennis E. Bills is an ordained minister in the Presbyterian Church in America. He received the Master of Arts in Theology from Bob Jones University and the Master of Education from Covenant College. He has preached with interpreters for ministries to internationals in the United States and throughout the Far East. Before becoming a pastor, he administrated Christian schools for ten years. He lives with his wife and three boys in West Virginia and loves to fish and hunt. His family's website is www.adoniram.net.